SERIOUS

WEIRD

TRUE 2
STORIES 2

Herbie Brennan

Illustrated by
David Wyatt

■SCHOLASTIC

Scholastic Children's Books,
Commonwealth House, 1–19 New Oxford Street
London WC1A 1NU, UK

A division of Scholastic Ltd
London ~ New York ~ Toronto ~ Sydney ~ Auckland

Published in the UK by Scholastic Ltd, 1998

Text copyright © Herbie Brennan, 1998
Illustrations copyright © David Wyatt, 1998

ISBN 0 590 19725 8

Typeset by Rapid Reprographics Ltd
Printed by Cox & Wyman Ltd, Reading, Berks

10 9 8 7 6 5 4 3 2 1

The right of Herbie Brennan and David Wyatt to be identified as the author
and illustrator of this work respectively has been asserted by them in
accordance with the Copyright, Designs and Patents Act, 1988.

CONTENTS

Introduction

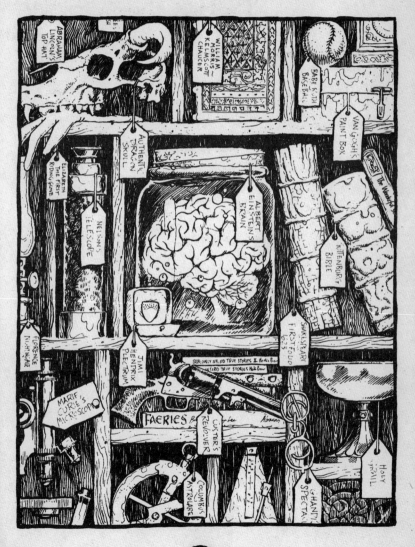

They're still at it.

In New Zealand, a black cat named Rastus has taken to riding a motor cycle. He climbs aboard with his owner, Max Corkill, and settles down on the handlebars while Max does the driving. To date, Rastus has bombed along the highways and byways of New Zealand for more than 150,000 miles. He wears a special helmet, goggles and (usually) a red spotted scarf for each trip.

In America, Citadel Press has published a book about what happens to bits of famous people after they die. The brain of the great physicist, Albert Einstein, was pickled. The religious mystic Emmanuel Swedenborg lost his head, which fortunately turned up later in a Welsh antique shop. Louis XIV's heart was eaten at a dinner party.

A growing number of experts are beginning to question whether NASA faked the (alleged?) moon landing of 1969. They point to really strange discrepancies in the published pictures – modules that landed without producing craters in the lunar dust, dark lunar skies without stars, shadows that suggest studio lighting and much more ... all adding up to one big question mark over that "giant leap for mankind".

At time of writing, police were still hunting for the Tickling Bandit who has been breaking into houses in Bendigo, Australia ... where he tickles children's feet. This is all he does. No one is hurt, no one attacked, nothing is stolen. The man normally gains access through an unlocked window. The Tickling Bandit first made his presence felt in 1990 and has struck 18 times since.

Nobody has yet suggested a connection between the

Tickling Bandit and the criminal currently being sought by the New York Police Department. Like his Australian counterpart, this character breaks into houses but never steals anything or harms anyone. Instead he makes porridge.

All these things are as seriously weird as anything recorded in the first book of this series (*Seriously Weird True Stories*, Scholastic, 1997) but they don't even start to tell you how weird things have got since that one was written.

For example, in *Seriously Weird* we mentioned how a woman was killed when an Airedale terrier fell on her head. You'd imagine that's about as weird a way to die as you could think of. But how about the World War One veterans who went one better when they managed to die of joy? They were awarded the coveted Legion D'Honneur to mark the 77th anniversary of the ending of hostilities and were so delighted they died while filling in the forms.

Seriously Weird told the story of the Green Children of Woolpit. Now a green cat has turned up in Denmark. It was discovered as a kitten in a hayloft by a woman named Pia Bischoff. Fur and claws are both green, but vets have pronounced the mog in excellent health. Experts are now wondering if the cat has an overdose of copper in its system. In neighbouring Sweden several blondes turned green due to drinking water contaminated by copper in corroded piping.

In this book, you'll find weirdnesses beyond your wildest dreams.

Like the mass lunacy that broke out in Europe ... all because of tulips!

Like those people past and present who can't be bothered to climb aboard an aeroplane when they want to fly, but simply float aloft without any mechanical aids whatsoever!

Like the tribes in Africa and Asia who claim ancestral

descent from alien life forms originating on a planet orbiting the star Sirius (8.7 light-years, or 51 trillion miles from Earth) … and have the evidence to prove it!

You'll learn about the boy who lived his entire life in water.

You'll discover that zombies really exist (and even find out how to make one).

You'll meet an Irish family in which four sons are more than twice as old as their mother.

In between these featured stories, you'll pay several visits to the Weird Zone – a collection of reports from right across the globe with just one thing in common: they demonstrate how dotty things can get.

And if your head isn't reeling already, you can turn the page now to investigate the incredibly weird story of the contest organized by three of the world's great Broadcasting Corporations … for singing mice!

The Great International
Mouse Singing Competition

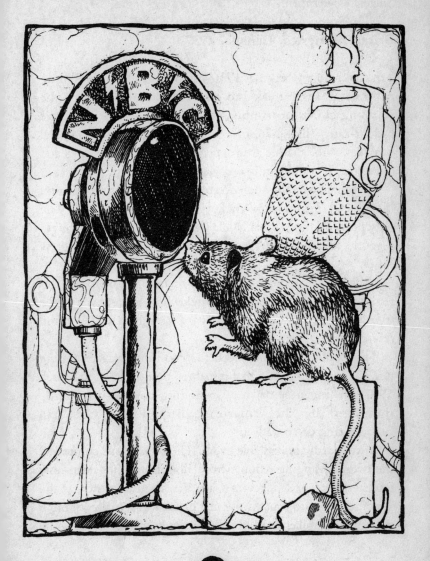

If you can never get out of bed early enough to hear the Dawn Chorus, take heart. At any time of day or night you might be serenaded by a rodent with ambitions to appear in The Great International Mouse Singing Competition...

Britain, America, Canada, 1937

Ten days before Christmas 1936, listeners to a Detroit, Illinois, radio station were treated to a remarkable new sound – the warbling chirps of Minnie, the singing mouse. The little rodent sang "like a robin" or, according to more cynical listeners, "like a tone deaf canary" but definitely sang and once started could hardly be persuaded to stop.

Encouraged by the audience reaction to Minnie, the station introduced her co-star (Mickey!) just three days later. The presenter announced that Mickey typically began singing with a gentle trill that built up to a climax, then gradually grew softer.

Unfortunately, the listeners had to take his word for this remarkable performance since Mickey got his feet wet while trying to drink water from a fruit jar, went into a decline and refused to sing at all.

This could easily have been the swansong of a promising new fad but for the fact that just three months later, in March 1937, an international mouse singing contest was jointly sponsored by the American, British and Canadian Broadcasting Corporations.

It was a truly remarkable event. The contestants comprised the original singing Minnie from Illinois and her until-now untested partner Mickey; a Canadian mouse known as the Toronto Tornado (but whose real name was actually Johnny); two English mice, both also confusingly called Mickey, one from London, the other from Devonport; and finally a Welsh mouse named Chrissie. Little is now known about the first four contestants, but there is some background on the other two.

Mickey from Devonport first appeared in the bedroom of Mrs Eddey of Stoke, in the opening minutes of New Year, 1937. He serenaded her, then disappeared, but returned on subsequent occasions and sometimes sang right throughout the night.

Mrs Eddey, who knew a good mouse when she heard one, set out to catch him and succeeded on the morning of 10 January. Despite his new life in captivity, Mickey continued to sing like a canary. "His little body positively vibrates with music," remarked Mrs Eddey.

Following some newspaper publicity, Mrs Eddey was approached by a Scots professor for permission to investigate the mouse scientifically, but Mickey's owner was more interested in having him broadcast. Early in March 1937, came the first indication that her ambitions might be realized. An executive from America's NBC, Miss Mildred Bontwood, sailed into Plymouth for the express purpose of giving Mickey an audition.

By this time the mouse had become quite tame. He was bundled into a cage and taken to the Plymouth studio of the BBC where he sang so effectively for Miss Bontwood that she issued Mrs Eddey with a broadcasting contract on his behalf. The arrangement was that, like Dick Whittington's cat, Mickey should go to London to take part in the Great International Mouse Singing Competition.

The following month marked the debut of Chrissie, the Welsh mouse, when her owner, Mrs Gale of Swansea, popped her into a bottle for her audition at the Swansea studios of the BBC. Chrissie "sang like a nightingale". Mrs Gale claimed Chrissie turned up a few days earlier than Devonport Mickey – at Christmas 1936 – but had disappeared only to turn up again inside a piano.

Despite the promise shown by these contestants, the Great International Mouse Singing Competition turned out to be a bit of a fiasco. Britain opened the batting with a duet between Mickey from Davenport and Chrissie from Swansea. It was an impressive performance but listeners afterwards complained that they could not tell the mice apart.

Illinois Mickey – whose feet had presumably dried out by this time – sang well, but Minnie, the original singing mouse of Illinois, became temperamental and refused to sing a note. Mickey from London performed so poorly that he was mistaken for a dripping tap. But the greatest disaster of all was the fate of the Toronto Tornado who was eaten (on air) by the studio cat.

Although the contest organizers solemnly promised that the top mice would appear live in an international mouse opera scheduled for later in the year, the winners of the Great International Mouse Singing Competition were never actually announced and remain a mystery to this day.

FACT FILE

1. Singing mice were known to Native Americans who called them Mish-a-boh-quas and believed their song was an omen of war. In Wiltshire folklore, the little warblers are supposed to warn of impending illness.

2. American author Arkady Fielder investigated an unusual species of fish in the Ucauali River which produced a noise like the ringing of bells. He published his findings in a book called *The River of the Singing Fish*.

3. A correspondent to *The Times* in 1937 put forward the theory that singing in mice was due to an affliction of the throat or bronchial tubes – in other words, the "song" was little more than a type of wheezing when the diseased mouse breathed deeply.

Other experts aren't so sure. They believe singing mice are actually imitating songbirds and are most likely to appear in a house that already has a budgie or a canary in good voice.

4. Singing mice are more common than most people imagine. The broadcasts in 1937 provoked several letters to the press from people with their own singing mouse stories to tell. The earliest recorded references to singing mice in Britain date back as far as 1857.

5. Dr Lee R. Dice, a zoologist at the University of Michigan, made the intriguing suggestion that all mice sing, but at a pitch too high for humans to hear them. Thus what we call singing mice are only those members of the species who happen to have bass voices.

6. Although they haven't taken part in broadcast competitions, there is some evidence to suggest the existence of singing rats, marmots and gophers.

The Boy Who Lived In Water

They say where you're brought up has a lot to do with the sort of person you become. But you'd hardly believe how far this could take you until you read about the boy who lived in water...

India, 1970s

Is it really possible to walk on water? An article appeared in *Probe India* in 1979 telling of a priest who claimed to have seen a naked boy do just that one afternoon in 1973.

The priest, from Baragdava, a village beside the little river Kuano in Uttar Pradesh, also saw the boy diving for and catching fish which he ate straight away. He was then carried downstream by the current, floating easily in the water.

According to Somni, an elderly woman from Baragdava, this boy was Ramchandra, her lost son, estimated to be about 15 years old, who had been swept away by the river when he was a 12-month-old baby.

There was only one further sighting before 1979 when the boy was finally caught and confirmed as Somni's son by the birthmark on his back. He was odd-looking with greenish black skin, almost no hair, unable to speak and, according to some reports, deaf. He got used to people and it became common to see him walking, and even running, on the water's surface; he could also stay under water far longer than normal human beings. He enjoyed catching and eating river prey, especially raw fish and frogs.

The villagers believed the river boy had supernatural origins, for Somni claimed the boy's father was an enormous being who appeared quite suddenly during a thunderstorm when she was on her way home from working in the family field. She said this being was like a spirit, that he had attacked her and then vanished as suddenly and as mysteriously as he had appeared. This spirit was thought to belong to a holy man who had drowned in a well he had dug many years earlier. Since he died while invoking the water goddess, it was believed he had claimed the boy for the water realm.

The story was investigated in 1985 by Hubert Adamson, who arrived in Gorakhpur, not far from the Nepalese border in Uttar Pradesh, only to discover that the water boy had died tragically three years earlier.

Apparently the boy had been arrested by two policemen but escaped back into the river. He travelled downstream, then headed for the town of Sanrigar, a short distance from the river by road.

It was night and the strange-looking boy apparently frightened a woman he approached in one of the roadside tea shops because she threw boiling water over him and he ran back to the river. It was the last time he was seen alive. His blistered, fish-bitten body was later found floating in the water.

The investigator wondered what might have provoked the police to attempt to hold him in the first place, when he had always been allowed to go about freely. He was told that Ramchandra had approached several village women and tried to embrace them. The unwelcome advances seem to have led to the police intervention.

1. There are numerous reports of other children who develop characteristics related to their upbringing. Berci Kutrovics of Hungary and Horst-Werner Reinhart of Germany were, for example, both reared by dogs and, when found, exhibited canine characteristics like walking on all fours, growling and sleeping curled up in a corner.

2. The idea that human beings might live comfortably in water is less far-fetched than it sounds. Babies in the womb live in a fluid environment and may be born quite safely under water since their oxygen supply continues to come from their mother for a short time at least after birth.

3. Most scientists agree that humans, in common with all mammals, evolved from primitive creatures that lived in the sea. But British naturalist Sir Alister Hardy went one better when he argued that our species returned to the water for a time at a relatively late stage of its evolution. This return, he claimed, left its mark in things like the way hair grows on our heads and bodies.

4. For centuries sailors throughout the world have added to a persistent mythology about human-like creatures living in water. Called mermaids or mermen, these beings are usually described as having a human appearance above the waist, but tapering to a fish tail below. Many scientists now believe the myth arose out of mistaken sightings of dugongs – large marine mammals that inhabit coastal waters from the Red Sea to northern Australia.

5. The idea that Ramchandra was fathered by a supernatural being provides a further link with worldwide mythology. Virtually every culture has its tales of heroes and oddities with supernatural parentage. In Britain the most familiar is the story of King Arthur's adviser, Merlin, whose father was a strange being with golden skin.

6. Ramchandra's skin colour was reminiscent of that of two English children, a brother and sister, caught in a wolf trap in medieval times. See the first *Seriously Weird* book for further details of these Green Children of Woolpit.

THE WEIRDZONE 1

The world gets weirder by the day. Here's our first presentation of the proof. Take a deep breath. You are about to enter the Weird Zone…

Is it a Bird? Is it a Plane? No, it's Muncherman!

America's Mort Hurst ate 16 double-decker moon pies in ten minutes and 38 eggs in 29 seconds in 1991. The feat earned him the title of Champion Eater … and resulted in his collapse from a blood clot on the brain. Fortunately he survived to run for the post of Secretary of State for North Carolina.

Hacking Cough

A tree that coughs at night has turned up in China. The maidenhair tree growing south-east of Beijing is over 80 feet high and nearly 50 feet in circumference. It is looked on as a living fossil and believed to be several thousand years old.

In April 1996, a passer-by heard the strange sound made by the tree – described as "like an old man coughing". Since he reported the phenomenon, thousands have flocked to the tree to hear it. Typically, the tree coughs several times in a night.

Priorities (1)

In Oklahoma you can be fined $5,000 for wrestling a bear, but only $2,000 for abusing your wife or husband.

Priorities (2)

Early in 1996, Greece and Turkey began to mass troops and warships in preparation for an open conflict over the island of Imia in the Aegean Sea. The total landmass of Imia covers no more than ten acres and the only things that can live there are goats. War was only averted by the timely intervention of international statesmen.

Election Fever

Tulsa, Oklahoma, held City Council elections in February 1996, but nobody at all voted in the 25th precinct. This came as no surprise to the authorities who are aware nobody has lived in the precinct for the past 20 years. Polling booths are opened for 12 hours each election on the off-chance somebody might turn up. If they did and were unable to vote, the entire election would be ruled invalid.

Keep Britain Tidy

A meeting of Bruntingthorpe Council in 1996 considered a plan to introduce DNA testing for the village's estimated 30 dogs. The results were to be kept on file so any dog dirt found on village streets could be matched with the animal that produced it and the dog's owner prosecuted.

A Taste for Drink

Sixty-year-old Philippe Delandtscheer has a special jail cell reserved for him in Lille, France. The authorities have realized he simply can't seem to stop stealing a particular type of aniseed flavoured liqueur. In 1996 he was accused of the offence … for the 51st time.

Throwing Money at the Problem

Alberto Ramirez was in a shop in Chatsworth, California, when a stranger approached him to ask for directions. Ramirez obliged, but to his surprise the man began to hurl abuse at him, then pelted him with items off the shelves.

Ramirez beat a hasty retreat from the shop, but the stranger followed and threw a knife at him. The weapon missed, but the man followed it up by throwing money. After a while, the stranger cooled down and drove away in a truck. Ramirez and others on the scene collected well over $2,000 from the pavement.

Good Manners

Russell Brown disturbed burglars in his Coventry home late one night, but mistook them for friends of the family and politely held open the door while they carried away electrical goods and other items. Russell, who was only four, was also kind enough to show them where to find his mother's purse and his father's power tools.

Bad Manners

In Houston, the capital of Texas, the Houston Metropolitan Transit Authority bans the carrying of concealed weapons by passengers on its buses. But not everyone agrees with what might seem a sensible enough precaution. In 1996, a Texan state senator named Jerry Patterson claimed he was thinking seriously of breaking the ban and threatened that if he did, he would then go to the Transit Authority and say, "Nah, nah, nah, nah! Rode your bus, rode your bus!"

Safer Smokes

Despite the massive amount of research linking cigarette smoking with lung cancer, the people of China (among others) remain massively addicted to the weed. But help is at hand. A Chinese inventor named Pu Danming has begun to market special "health cigarettes" in Beijing. Each cigarette contains herbs, a small battery and a microchip. You don't actually light it but when you take a puff an LED glows at the end as if you had and the cigarette plays a patriotic tune.

Safer Hangings

Non-slip safety strips were fixed to the steps of the latest gallows to be constructed at the Delaware Correctional Centre in the United States to make sure convicted murderer Billy Bailey didn't slip and hurt himself while going to be hanged in 1996.

High-tech Homeless

Neal Berry, a 22-year-old Californian man, sleeps by the side of the road, but runs a portable computer, a cellular phone, a personal postbox and an e-mail account. He rents a storage locker for his belongings and has taken out a membership of a local gym so he can shower in the mornings. Mr Berry works as a shipping clerk.

Smelling a Rat

There's now worldwide interest in an imaginative new development by the Sigma Chemical Company – artificial pongs.

Sigma have created scents that mimic the smell of dead bodies. They're even able to produce scents that differentiate between bodies less than and more than a month old. (They're called, appropriately, Pseudo Corpse I and Pseudo Corpse II.) They also have on offer the smell of drowning and burns victims, not to mention the spectacular scent of somebody alive but in shock (Pseudo Distressed Body).

These novel perfumes are used mainly to train dogs to locate accident victims.

Loony Tulips

Take care next time you pick a tulip. Holland's national flower can do strange things to people. Just look what happened when it first got popular…

The Netherlands, 17th century

In 1559, a German gentleman named Conrad Gesner was visiting a garden in Augsburg when he spotted a small planting of most unusual flowers. When he asked his host, a scholar named Counsellor Herwart, what type of blooms they were, he was told they were tulips, a rare bulb imported from Constantinople where the flower had been popular for many years.

This is the first recorded reference to tulips anywhere in Western Europe … and the beginning of a weirdness so extreme that doctors now suspect it must have been a form of mania.

Herr Gesner liked the tulips when he saw them. He was not the only one. In the months that followed, more and more visitors piled into the Herwart garden and while it was packed with many exotic plant species, it was the tulips everyone came to see.

Before long, other plant collectors were sending to Constantinople for tulip bulbs of their own. Within ten years, tulips had become the most sought-after flowers in Germany and Holland – at least among the wealthy, who were the only people able to afford them.

But that was just the beginning. The first tulips to find their way into England arrived in the year 1600, imported from Vienna. They were already very expensive, yet each year for the next 34 years they became more expensive still. Despite the price tag, they also became more popular. By 1634, it was actually considered an act of bad taste for any wealthy person to be without a tulip collection.

From 1634 onwards, the passion for tulips spread. Everybody who was anybody had to have as many tulips as they could possibly afford in their garden, however much hardship the purchase of the rare flowers caused them.

And hardship there was. Around this time, a Dutch merchant sold half of everything he possessed in order to buy a single tulip bulb. The weird thing was he didn't do this in the hope of turning a profit when he sold the flower again. He wanted the tulip for his conservatory where it could be admired by his friends.

This merchant was by no means unusual. The obsession with tulips had grown to such an extent in the Netherlands that the entire economy of the country began to suffer. People abandoned their normal employment in their scores, in their hundreds and finally in tens of thousands ... in order to buy and sell tulips.

The price of bulbs had by now gone through the roof. A batch of 40 roots cost in the region of 100,000 florins, an enormous sum of money in today's values. Tulips were so expensive that they could no longer be sold by the bunch, or even by the bulb. Instead they were sold by the *perit*, a measure something less than the weight of a grain of corn.

But weight wasn't everything. The species of tulip made a huge difference to the price. For example, an *Admiral Van der Eyck* tulip weighing 446 perits would sell at 1,260 florins, while a *Semper Augustus* at less than half the weight would set you back a massive 5,500 florins. To give you some idea of the money values of the time, a florin would be worth between £3 and £5 today in general purchasing power.

In the early months of 1636, 12 acres of prime building

land were offered for one bulb, while somebody else handed over a brand-new carriage, two matched grey horses, a set of harnesses and 4,600 florins for another.

Even these trades paled into insignificance when placed against the following delivery to the tulip mart: four oxen, eight pigs, 12 sheep, two hogsheads of wine, four tons of beer, two tons of butter, 450 kg of cheese, one bed, one suit of clothes, one silver drinking cup and substantial quantities of wheat and rye. The delivery bought one bulb of the *Viceroy* tulip species.

With so many people engaged in the buying and selling of tulips, it comes as no surprise to discover that the great trading houses in Amsterdam, Rotterdam and other Dutch centres eventually devoted so much of their energies to tulip selling that nearly everything else was forgotten. A new profession of tulip-jobbers came into existence, men who made a living by speculating on the rise and fall of tulip prices. Many did more than simply make a living. Since the price had risen steadily for years, they made a fortune.

By about 1610 a single bulb of a new variety was acceptable as a bride's dowry. In France, a flourishing brewery was exchanged for one bulb of the variety *Tulipe Brasserie*.

Encouraged by this, the population of Holland as a whole succumbed to tulip mania. Everybody believed the price of tulips would go on rising forever. There was confidence that the wealthy and fashionable of Europe would continue to buy the bulbs at whatever cost. There was a rash of selling as people converted their property into cash – often far below its actual value – which they promptly invested in the precious flowers. Even houses and land were sold. Holland had turned into one vast get-rich-quick machine and from the noblest aristocrat to the most humble peasant, everybody was determined to get in on the act.

Incredibly, the action grew more frenzied. Tulip mania was now sweeping the whole of Europe and since the Netherlands was the undisputed centre of the tulip trade, money began to flow into the country from abroad in torrents. Property increased in value. Prices generally began to rise. Nobody cared. In a matter of months, it seemed, Holland had become the wealthiest country in the world. A bandwagon had begun to roll and just about everybody was aboard.

Tulip trading was now so widespread and involved such a sophisticated system of cash, credit and barter payments that the government found it necessary to draw up an entire code of laws for the guidance of the dealers. Special notaries and clerks were appointed whose sole occupation was the administration of the trade.

In towns without stock exchanges, tulip trading took place in the inns and taverns. This led to a tradition of celebratory banquets to mark particularly satisfying deals – and most tulip deals were particularly satisfying in those days. Anything up to 300 people would sit down to these celebrations. At intervals along the tables would be set vases of the priceless tulips.

So it went, week on week, month on month until, suddenly, the market collapsed. Modern commentators believe the trigger was a crisis of confidence. Nobody was buying tulips to keep any more, only to resell at a profit. Anybody with half an eye could see that an awful lot of people were going to lose money once the frenzy stopped. A trickle of people decided to cut their losses and get out. In days the trickle became a torrent, then a flood.

Inevitably, fortunes were lost even more quickly than they'd been made. Many merchants and even nobles were brought to their financial knees. There was instant panic. Those with stocks of now almost worthless tulips called public meetings throughout Holland and sent messengers to the government, calling for action. The government declined to take any, almost certainly because it had no idea what to do.

In desperation the crisis was referred to the most revered body in the land, the Provincial Council at the Hague. The members deliberated for three months … then asked for more information.

It was, of course, the end of tulip lunacy in Holland. As news of the disaster spread, tulip markets collapsed in Britain, France and other European countries. Here the mania had not run nearly so high, but all the same many fortunes were still lost.

1. At the height of the tulip mania in Holland, a sailor ate a 3,000-florin *Semper Augustus* bulb, mistaking it for an onion.

2. A 17th-century Dutch author named Munting wrote a detailed, 1,000-page description of the tulip mania – a feat almost as loony as the mania itself.

3. In London in the year 1800, you could be asked to pay 15 guineas for a single tulip bulb – roughly equivalent to a servant's wage for five years.

4. As late as 1835, a tulip of the species *Miss Fanny Kemble* went under the auctioneer's hammer in Britain for £75 while a Chelsea market garden valued one of its prize blooms at 200 guineas, the price of a house and grounds.

5. Botanists recognize about 100 species of tulip altogether. Although the flowers grow wild as far afield as Japan, two thirds of all species are native to the eastern Mediterranean.

6. Since the high days of tulip mania, horticulturists have managed to develop almost 4,000 varieties, reflecting the fact that tulips to this day are among the most popular of all garden flowers.

The Blob From Beyond

Scientists once believed stones couldn't possibly fall from the sky. Then they discovered meteorites. But stones aren't the only things to fall from the sky … and some of them are very difficult to explain.

Canada, 1979

It was Saturday 16 June, a hot summer's afternoon, when Donna Matchett was busy cleaning the swimming pool at the back of the family home in Mississauga, Ontario, Canada.

Suddenly something landed with a thud on the picnic table behind her. Assuming it was the dog thumping his tail on the decking, she didn't look round until she heard a cracking sound. Her scream alerted her father, Traven, who was doing a paint job nearby. They both watched as a column of flame shot upwards like a blowtorch from a molten mass in the middle of the table.

After standing paralysed for a moment, Donna hurriedly doused the flame with the garden hose. Later, Traven Matchett described some peculiarities of the flame. He described it as very intense, about 46 cms high and completely cylindrical. Both he and Donna insisted the 20-mm–diameter flame was flat on top. Once extinguished, the molten mass shrank to a pitted dark green solid weighing about 113 grammes.

A call to the control tower of nearby Toronto International Airport confirmed that the flaming blob could not have come from a passing plane as an aircraft would have needed to be on fire to have dropped something that hot. Public uproar followed a report in the *Sunday Sun* the next day and soon the story was spreading across Canada.

Ministry of Environment analysis concluded that the substance was polypropylene, a common chemical plastic used in making many household objects, including Frisbees, which according to the Ministry inspector was the most likely identity of the mystery blob. But Matchett was not impressed by the flaming Frisbee theory and set about testing it by setting light to a couple of Frisbees of his own. The results were quite different to, and far less spectacular than, the way the mystery blob had burned.

Following the press reports Traven Matchett was contacted by three other people, one from only 1.5 km away and two from nearby Brampton, all of whom claimed to have had mysterious blobs appearing in their backyards. The largest weighed in the region of 3.6 kg.

FACT FILE

1. It's only relatively recently that scientists have believed *anything* could fall from the sky, let alone mysterious blobs. In the 18th century, a spokesman for the Academy of Sciences stated categorically that "stones cannot fall from the sky because there are no stones in the sky". When shown a meteorite he decided the stone had been in the ground all along but had been unearthed by lightning.

2. Blobs of stuff – but presumably not polypropylene – have been reported as falling from the skies for centuries. There's even a name for the material, which typically decomposes quickly with a particularly bad smell. It's called *pewtr ser* or the "rot of the stars" and has been found, usually in rural areas, in Great Britain, parts of Europe and America, with reports going back as far as the 17th century.

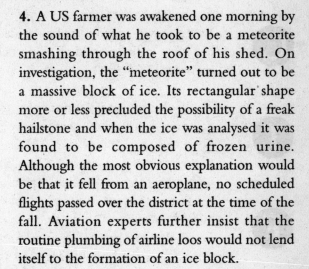

3. Freak weather conditions can produce hailstones large enough to smash their way through roofs of houses and even cause serious dents in the metal bodywork of cars. In some cases, people have been killed by a single hailstone.

4. A US farmer was awakened one morning by the sound of what he took to be a meteorite smashing through the roof of his shed. On investigation, the "meteorite" turned out to be a massive block of ice. Its rectangular shape more or less precluded the possibility of a freak hailstone and when the ice was analysed it was found to be composed of frozen urine. Although the most obvious explanation would be that it fell from an aeroplane, no scheduled flights passed over the district at the time of the fall. Aviation experts further insist that the routine plumbing of airline loos would not lend itself to the formation of an ice block.

5. The noted ichthyologist (fish scientist), Dr E. W. Gudger of the American Museum of Natural History in New York, published five learned papers on fish between 1921 and 1946. But the fish he studied didn't swim in the sea – they fell as heavy rains from the sky.

6. Ancient Egyptian and Graeco-Roman texts make reference to a substance called "foam of the moon", a white stone like glass which can be rubbed into fragments and used for magical purposes. There are several theories about the nature of this stone and while many experts believe it to have been created in the primitive processes of early chemists and alchemists, there remains the possibility that it was a (possibly meteoric) substance that fell from the sky.

Can They Be Sirius?

There are people around who claim their ancestors arrived on Earth by flying saucer. Not all of them appear to be nuts.

Africa, early 1930s; Asia, today

In 1931, two French scientists specializing in the study of how people live moved in with a Sudanese tribe called the Dogon. Like many tribal people, the Dogon had two religions – the faith practised by the common people and special teachings known only to a special few.

Fifteen years after joining the life of the tribe, one of the scientists, Marcel Griaule, got to learn the special teachings. The secrets that were revealed to him proved quite extraordinary, for they had little to do with the sort of tribal creation myths you might expect. Instead, they were to do with astronomy.

Griaule discovered that Dogon secret doctrine, dating back countless generations in the history of the tribe, taught that the Earth and planets orbited the sun – something unknown in Europe until the publication of Copernicus's *De Revolutionibus Orbium Caelestium* ("On the Revolutions of the Heavenly Spheres") in 1543. Before then, everyone in Europe believed the Earth was the centre of the universe and the sun and planets were in orbit around it.

The Dogon were aware of the moons of Jupiter, invisible to the naked eye. Galileo discovered the same thing in 1609 following the invention of the telescope, but the Dogon religion was being taught centuries before then.

The Dogon also knew about the rings of Saturn, first interpreted by Christian Huygens, the greatest observational astronomer, in 1659. They were aware the moon was a dead, dry airless body and had records of the movements of Venus –

something else that wasn't known in Europe until the time of Galileo.

But the real surprise the Dogon had for their French friend was the ancient story that the star Sirius had a tiny companion which was dark, dense and very, very heavy. The reason for its weight was that it was composed of matter heavier than any found on Earth. It moved in an elliptical orbit which it took 50 years to complete.

It was not unexpected that the Dogon should have noticed Sirius. It is, after all, the brightest star in the night sky. But the idea of an invisible companion was something else. It was only in 1834 that the German astronomer Friedrich Bessel noticed that Sirius moved in a peculiar way and decided the only explanation had to be an invisible companion. In 1862, Alvan Clark discovered that companion, now called Sirius B, using a large, sophisticated telescope.

In 1928 (just three years before the scientists visited the Dogon) Sir Arthur Eddington came up with the idea of white dwarfs — stars that are nearing the end of their lives and growing smaller as they burn out. Several hundred white dwarfs are now known. One of them is Sirius B. It's about the size of planet Earth and it weighs as much as the sun. It has an orbit that takes 50 years to complete.

There's absolutely nothing in Dogon culture to provide a logical explanation of how the tribal initiates came by this accurate and detailed information. They do not practise astronomy and even if they did, it is difficult to see how they could have worked it all out without powerful telescopes and/or an advanced knowledge of astrophysics.

The Dogon themselves claim the knowledge was given to them by a god who came down to Earth from Sirius (or a planet circling Sirius) and founded the Dogon nation.

The Dogon aren't the only ones to claim they came from outer space, especially the Sirius star system. The Dropa, or Dzopa, a tribe from the remote mountains of Baian-Kara-Ula on the borders of Tibet and China also say they came from Sirius. With large knobby heads, small bodies barely 1.3 metres tall, they certainly look odd enough to be space people.

Scientists first got interested in the Dropa back in 1938, when tiny human bones were found in a large cave system in the Baian-Kara-Ula mountains. Along with these carefully buried skeletons (with unusually large skulls) Chinese archaeologists found many stone discs, dated from around 10,000 BC, each with a circular hole at the centre and spiral grooves on the surface. As many as 716 discs were discovered in one cave. The scientists thought they might work like a gramophone record or a CD-ROM. The problem was figuring out how to use them.

The secret of the discs remained a mystery until 1962, when a professor, Dr Tsum Um Nui of the Peking Academy of Prehistory, finally broke the code. It took two years for the Academy to agree that he could publish his findings. They were very weird findings indeed. The professor concluded that the information on the discs related to a spaceship that landed on Earth 12,000 years ago.

One small segment of the discs read:

The Dropa came out of the clouds in their aeroplanes. Before sunrise, our men, women and children hid in the caves ten times. When they finally understood the sign language of the Dropa, they realized the newcomers had peaceful intentions…

Another part said that the Han people (who lived in nearby caves and now make up the majority of the Chinese population) regretted that the Dropa had crashed in such a remote place and couldn't build a new craft to return to their home planet.

Unfortunately for the professor, his paper wasn't taken seriously. He was dismissed as a crank or a fraud and moved to Japan a year later.

During the years since the discs were discovered more has been learnt about the Baian-Kara-Ula area. Much of it backs up Dr Tsum Um Nui's findings. Local legend tells how short, thin, yellow men "had come out of the clouds a very long time ago". Wall paintings depicting the sunrise, the moon, unknown stars and the Earth, all connected with dotted lines, were found inside a cave. The caverns of the Baian-Kara-Ula are still inhabited by the Han and the Dropa tribes and the Dropa are neither Tibetan nor Chinese racial types.

Russian scientists got hold of some of the Dropa discs and discovered that they contained a variety of metals including large amounts of cobalt. *Sputnik* magazine published a report by Dr Viatcheslav Saisev saying that, when placed on a machine something like a gramophone, the discs vibrated as if they had an electrical charge.

Two of the discs seem to have ended up in China's Banpo Museum. In 1994 two experts, Hartwig Hausdorf and Peter Krassa, went to China in the hope of tracing them. They visited the museum but found nothing. Their official guides and the museum director all denied any knowledge of such discs. But eventually, after being shown photographs, the Director, Professor Wang Zhijun, admitted the discs did exist – or at least *had* existed – but a former director who allowed them to be photographed had been forced to resign and had since disappeared.

A few years ago Professor Zhijun was told by his superiors

that all traces of the discs had to be wiped out and he was to claim any references to them were lies.

The discs were also investigated by an Englishman, Dr Karyl Robin-Evans, who went to China in 1947 after being shown a stone disc supposedly found in northern India. He was told that the disc had belonged to the Dropa tribe and was used in their religious ceremonies. It was believed to lose and gain weight over a period of three-and-a-half hours.

Intrigued by the story, Robin-Evans travelled to Lhasa in Tibet, then continued on into the high border mountains of Baian-Kara-Ula. Eventually he reached the Dropa and stayed long enough to learn their language and the history of the tribe. Lurgan-La, the tribe's religious leader, told him that the Dropa came from Sirius and that two Sirian expeditions had been sent to Earth, one more than 20,000 years ago and another in AD 1014. His tribe were, he said, the descendants of the second visit when several ships had crashed and been unable to return home.

This information doesn't tally with the information Dr Tsum Um Nui claimed he found on the discs, so it's clear the last word hasn't been written about the Dropa, but at least one more expedition is planned in an attempt to clear up the mystery.

FACT FILE

1. Sirius is also known as Alpha Canis Majoris, the Dog Star, and has given its name to the Dog Days, periods of exceptionally hot and humid weather that often occur in July, August and early September in northern latitudes. Several ancient peoples believed that Sirius added its heat to that of the sun, thus causing the hot weather.

2. Sirius was particularly important to the ancient Egyptians since its appearance in the night sky heralded the beginning of the annual Nile floods. They used Sirius to correct their inaccurate lunar calendar: Sirius returns yearly, give or take just 12 minutes.

3. A special ceremony called the sigui marks the climax of Dogon religious life. The ceremony is held when Sirius appears between two mountain peaks – something that occurs just once in every 60 years. Before the ritual, young men go into seclusion for three months, during which they speak a secret language.

4. The Sirius mystery is not the only peculiar thing about the Dogon. There is some doubt as to the correct classification of their language. Different experts have placed it in several different language groups, showing the difficulty of tracing Dogon origins.

5. The idea of extraterrestrial contact is widespread among many different cultures. From the ancient Middle East to the modern-day Australian Aborigines, it is common to find myths of racial origins in outer space or visitations from alien beings. Since the myths are almost invariably couched in religious terms – "heaven" or "beyond the sky" standing for outer space, "gods", "angels" or "sky spirits" referring to the visitors and so on – it is only relatively recently that some observers have begun to wonder how literally these stories should be taken.

6. Recently theories have been put forward that the existence of the Dropa may account for persistent legends about "secret masters", advanced cultures or a race of supermen hidden away in the remote vastness of Tibet. These legends inspired the English novelist James Hilton to write his highly-successful work *Lost Horizon* which tells of a secret paradise in the Tibetan valley of Shangri-la.

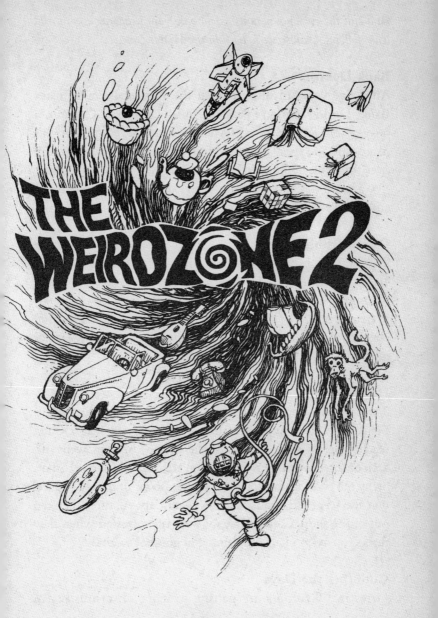

THE WEIRDZONE 2

And still the evidence mounts. Hold onto your headgear as you read what follows, because we're back in the Weird Zone...

Bank Deposit

After five years in dispute with the National Westminster Bank, David Cannon's patience finally gave out. Cannon, a 66-year-old farmer from Newcastle, England, coupled up his silage tank and spray deposited four tons of liquid cow manure over the bank building. The mess took two weeks to clean.

Cannon was subsequently convicted of criminal damage and received a hefty fine.

Dumb Robbers (1)

Thieves who broke into a huge commercial freezer at Spring Valley, California, in 1996 thought they were stealing steaks belonging to a nearby gourmet restaurant. They weren't. When officials of the Paradise Valley Road Pet Hospital checked the freezer next morning, they discovered the bodies of nine dead dogs had gone missing.

Dumb Robbers (2)

Three teenage robbers hit a supermarket in Miami, Florida, in February 1996. As one of them, 18-year-old Jeanis Caty, reached across the counter for the money, his gun went off, accidentally shooting his companion, 16-year-old Wesley Steny. Steny fell back against the third robber (so far unnamed) whose gun also went off, accidentally shooting Caty. All three then ran out of the shop. Caty and Steny were later arrested when they turned up at hospital complaining of gunshot wounds.

Counting the Days

Juries in Oklahoma are getting tougher on criminals. In

March 1996, one defendant was sentenced to 11,250 years in jail, while another received a sentence of 21,250 years.

But even these terms were small fry compared with the sentence handed down in 1994 and confirmed on appeal two years later. That one put away a criminal for 30,000 years.

Going Crackers

A 22-year-old employee of America's Wolpac company took a Ritz cracker at lunch belonging to a 26-year-old co-worker … who went home for his .38-calibre handgun, then came back and opened fire on the thief. Fortunately he was subdued before any real harm was done.

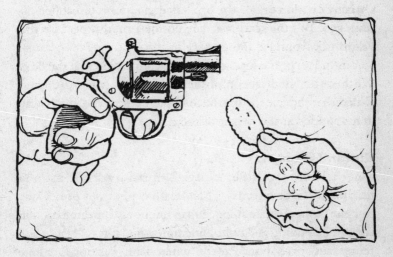

Beer and Crackers

In the same month as the Wolpac incident, a US rancher was so appalled to be served warm beer in an American Legion club that he returned armed with two rifles and took customers hostage. The crisis was not resolved for nine hours, during which a police officer was killed.

Look After the Pennies

Canadian Salim Kara was 31 when he came up with an unusual money-making sideline. He started stealing coins from slot machines using a rod with a magnet on the end.

Thirteen years later, the law finally caught up with him when he bought an $800,000 home despite the fact his salary as a transit worker was only $38,000 a year. Police discovered he had extracted an astonishing $2.3 million from the slot machines. Kara was sentenced to four years' imprisonment.

Close Enough for Rock

In 1996, the controversial pop group, The Sex Pistols, planned a special reunion tour – the first since the group disbanded 20 years ago. But the tour was delayed for a month because the Pistols now sounded too good.

Virgin Records issued a statement confirming that the boys had become such accomplished musicians since the band folded that they needed practice to get back to the grotty way they sounded at the height of their fame.

Korean Colour

On 16 February 1996, North Korean leader Kim Jong reached his 54th birthday ... and nature went out of her way to help him celebrate. Concentric rainbows appeared around the sun defending and upholding him while it was "bright and temperate" on Mount Paektu, where Kim was born, despite the fact that the temperature had averaged 40° below zero for the past century.

The information was given to the world by the official North Korean news agency, which added that the weather on Kim's birthday had been bright and temperate each year since the day he was born.

Lightning Cure

Mary Clamser of Oklahoma City suffered from multiple sclerosis, a disease of the brain and spinal cord that gradually destroys the myelin covering of nerve fibres, eventually resulting in permanent paralysis. Since medical science has not yet found the cause of this disease, it is currently considered incurable.

Except that Mary Clamser seems to have been cured by lightning. She was grasping metal objects in each hand and wearing a metal leg brace when lightning struck her home in 1994. Immediately afterwards, she began to walk easily.

Lightning Writer

Brazilian Ryoki Inoue finished his 1,039th novel in 1996. Watched by a newspaper reporter, he started the book around 10 p.m. one evening and by 5.30 next morning he had completed a 195-page thriller about drug traffickers and corrupt cops.

Mr Inoue started writing just ten years ago.

Who Watched their Coats?

About 100 criminals attended the world's first Muggers' Convention in Bangladesh in the spring of 1996. Members elected their leader a "Master Hijacker" in honour of his feat of achieving 21 muggings in two hours and decided the city of Dhaka was now sufficiently prosperous to warrant their doubling the number of muggings there.

Wrestling with Injury

In 1991, Sarah M. Milliken suffered back injuries when her car skidded on an icy patch in Pennsylvania.

In 1996, Ms Milliken sued the Pennsylvania Department of

Transportation on the grounds that her injuries had not got better. But the case was thrown out of court when the defence produced a videotape showing Ms Milliken in a bathing suit wrestling with another woman in a vat of coleslaw during a Biker Week in Florida just a year after her accident.

Flying Nuns
and Other (Human) UFOs

Lots of people are afraid of flying in aeroplanes. Now they've got something new to worry about. The possibility of flying without them.

Various locations, 16th century to present day

Saint Teresa of Avila was supposed to have reached such states of ecstasy that she actually levitated. According to the *Sunday People* a nun named only as Sister Rosa was doing much the same thing in 1977.

Sister Anne of the Incarnation saw St Teresa of Avila floating about half a metre off the ground when she was in a state of holy rapture. The saint could not stop the levitation which occurred despite her resistance and frightened her enormously.

Saint Teresa was not the only follower of a religious vocation to find herself transported on high. St Joseph of Cupertino was a famous 17th-century flyer who, it was recorded, always gave a peculiar little shriek just before taking off.

Sister Rosa, the modern levitating nun, was the centre of a mass of flying activity which involved both her own levitation and other objects flying around her.

On one occasion she was watched by her terrified sisters as she floated up through the ceiling and was afterwards found standing on the floor above. Another time, she was found screaming. Investigation showed thorns from a cactus plant in the garden were embedded in her skull beneath her cowl.

Once she was beaten by an iron bar that had detached itself from the outside of her door, travelled through the wall and rematerialized to attack her in her cell.

Levitation is a weirdness associated with a whole range of

paranormal experience – shamanistic trance, possession, mystical ecstasy, mediumship and hauntings. Although flying Christians are best known to our Western culture, the other major world religions claim their share of gravity defying phenomena. Japanese ninja are supposed to be able to levitate as one of their secret practices. The famous 13th-century Tibetan yogi, Milarepaas was supposed to be able to sleep as well walk when levitating.

Photographs taken from all angles exist of Subbayah Pullavar, a famous Indian fakir from Tinnivelly, floating in a horizontal position about a metre above the ground. His only support is one hand resting lightly on a cloth-wrapped stick. At the time the photographs were taken, well over a hundred eyewitnesses verified the performance, which lasted about four minutes. A particular branch of yoga practice was apparently traditional in the Pullavar family for generations.

This ties in with the Eastern tradition of using breathing and visualization techniques to manipulate universal life-force energy, called *chi, ki* or *prana,* to cause effects like levitation, although it's difficult to see why a stick would be needed. The circumstances are made even more suspicious by the fact that stage conjurers routinely demonstrate a similar "levitation" supported by a single rod, or sometimes sword.

A French judge, Louis Jacolliot, explored these mysteries in his book *Occult Science in India and Among the Ancients,* where he describes being told by Brahmins that the "supreme cause" of these paranormal effects was the *agasa,* that is "the moving thought of the universal soul, directing all souls" which experts learn to control. Jacolliot also had this to say about a floating fakir:

Taking an ironwood cane which I had brought from Ceylon [Sri

Lanka], he leaned heavily upon it, resting his right hand upon the handle, with his eyes fixed upon the ground. He then proceeded to utter the appropriate incantations … [and] rose gradually about two feet from the ground.

His legs were crossed beneath him, and he made no change in his position, which was very like that of those bronze statues of Buddha … For more than 20 minutes I tried to see how [he] could thus fly in the face and eyes of all known laws of gravity … the stick gave him no visible support, and there was no apparent contact between that and his body, except through his right hand.

Apart from cases endorsed by the Church, levitation in the West has often been viewed as an evil and, from medieval times, usually associated with witchcraft and demonic possession. Levitation is still fairly widely reported in cases of so-called possession, where objects as well as people are said to fly through the air, and holy water is then used as an antidote.

It's an antidote that certainly worked in the case of Clara Germana Cele, a South African schoolgirl, who floated a metre or so in the air until a sprinkling with holy water made her fall. This result was taken as proof that she had been demonically possessed.

D. D. Home was the most famous medium to levitate. It is reported that, in 1868 in London, he floated outside through an open third-floor window, was seen in mid-air outside another window, through which he returned inside, only to shoot head-first back outside again via the original window before finally returning to the room feet-first.

Recent cases of "yogic flying" have been widely reported in relation to the advanced practice of transcendental meditation. This takes the form of low hops made while seated cross-legged in the lotus position and is supposed to happen as a result of specially ordered brain wave activity, enabling the practitioner to tap into the "unified field" of cosmic energy.

1. The levitation of witches (who were supposed in folklore to fly on broomsticks) is called transvection and believed to involve a special "flying ointment" rubbed on their bodies. Historical investigation shows "flying ointments" actually existed and contained potent plant drugs which caused their users to fall into a trance and *dream* of flying.

2. The essential difference between the type of levitation supposedly practised by witches and that practised by saints, is that saints have always flown directly upwards as if trying to reach heaven, while witches were supposed to levitate in order to get to somewhere else on Earth.

3. Modern psychical research classified levitation under the general heading of psychokinesis – influencing matter by the power of the mind. In levitation, the matter influenced is the body of the levitator and the question arises as to why people who can levitate themselves can't seem to levitate other people or objects.

4. Scientists recently reported that when electricity was run through a certain type of coil, objects above it lost weight. The scientists can't agree why this happens (or even if it happens all the time) but some of them believe the coil may have screened out a little of the planet's gravity. If this idea is true, all you need to do is build a bigger and better coil and the result will be the world's first anti-gravity machine … which will allow anyone (and anything) to levitate.

5. An English traveller in northern India during the 1930s claims he witnessed a group of priests levitate a large block of stone by chanting at it.

6. Investigation into the levitation phenomenon is confused by the fact that this is one of the easiest of all apparently mystical powers to fake through conjuring. In the classical version of the illusion, a woman lies on a table and is covered with a cloth before rising, apparently without support, about a metre into the air. Often a metal hoop is passed all around her to "prove" there are no hidden wires. The trick is done by an hydraulic lift hidden from the audience, which lifts the woman, table top and all. The really clever bit is the U-shaped connection between the lift and the table which allows the conjurer to give the impression that he's passing the hoop all the way round when, in fact, he's doing nothing of the sort.

The Day
of the Living Dead

Remember those stupid late night TV horror movies where voodoo priests dug up corpses in Haiti and turned them into zombies? Maybe they weren't so stupid after all.

Haiti, 1986

Seventeen-year-old Andre Ville Jean-Paul had a lot to look forward to. He'd fallen in love, proposed to the girl of his dreams, been accepted and was engaged to be married. Although he lived in Haiti, a poor Caribbean republic, he had work to do and prospects for the future.

Then one day, without warning, he suffered what appeared to be an epileptic fit. He felt himself spiral downwards into a deep, dark emptiness.

Andre's family thought he was dead. They made the funeral arrangements quickly, as is the custom in Haiti where the heat encourages early decomposition of a body. Andre was placed in a casket and solemnly buried.

But he wasn't dead and even burial didn't kill him. He lay in a sort of trance, unable to move, but aware of his surroundings and what was going on. He knew, to his horror, he was in a coffin. He knew he was underground. Worst of all, he knew he could do nothing about it. He was hot, hungry and filthy, but he could not so much as flicker an eyelid to help himself get out.

The horror lasted, by his own estimate, about two weeks. Then, as unexpectedly as his original seizure, Andre's coffin began to move. He felt it rise up through the earth and heard a stern voice order him to stand. His body tingled, but he could do nothing. The voice repeated the order and he felt a limb twitch. For a third time the mystery voice ordered him to rise and Andre found himself climbing out of the casket.

But his body felt strange, as if it was no longer under his own control.

Andre was surrounded by a group of figures who beat him and marked him with a knife before they sold him to a *houngan*, the local name for a voodoo priest. The *houngan* also beat him, then put him to work on a plantation with nearly a score of other zombies.

The entire group was treated as slave labour. They had to work naked under the supervision of a dwarf who wore a belt of bells. They received no money and little rest. Their diet consisted of bananas, rice and unsalted meat which their owner claimed was human flesh. They were given a strong distilled alcoholic spirit to drink.

The reason their meat was unsalted was an ancient tradition that the taste of salt would break the spell that held the zombies captive. But in Andre's case it was broken anyway, although not until he had slaved for several years.

One afternoon in the boiling sun, a member of the zombie group seemed to go insane and beat the priest to death. With the *houngan* dead, the remaining zombies, including Andre, emerged from their trance. He discovered to his amazement he was no longer a teenage boy, but a fully-grown man, although he had no real idea how many years he had worked in the Haitian fields.

Andre emerged from his ordeal in the spring of 1993, seven years after he had "died" – and promptly became famous because of it. Local entrepreneurs turned him into a sort of zombie celebrity and arranged for him to tell his story in public at special gatherings. So many turned up that the organizers were forced to hire a football field in Port-au-Prince to accommodate them.

The Haitian authorities stepped in. To them, large crowds

meant the possibility of revolution – Haiti's government was none too popular at the time. They insisted Andre's people kept him on the move so that his appearances became impromptu events without prior publicity.

It made no difference to the size of the crowds. If anything, Andre's fame spread further and faster than ever. People began to recognize him in the street. Crowds would gather around him as if he were a pop singer. Everybody wanted to touch him. It's considered lucky to touch a zombie in Haiti.

Andre is not the only zombie to return from the (living) dead and tell the tale. A northern Haitian peasant named Clerveus Narcisse was pronounced dead and buried near his home in May 1962. But in January 1980, Clerveus turned up again sporting a hole in his right cheek which he claimed had been made by a coffin nail. He claimed he had spent the intervening 18 years working as a zombie on a voodoo priest's plantation.

Can we take these stories seriously? The Haitian authorities certainly do. A life sentence was imposed in March 1989 on a defendant convicted of creating a zombie. But how did he go about it?

Haitian tradition has it that zombies are created by voodoo, a much maligned and misunderstood creed that is in all but name the official religion of Haiti. Outside the island, voodoo is often considered to be a term more or less synonymous with black magic. But nothing could be further from the truth. The basis of voodoo is spiritualist African beliefs, imported with the slave trade and mixed with elements of French Catholicism. (France was the colonial power in Haiti until the island achieved independence in 1804.)

The religion falls into the category of ecstatic. That's to say, voodoo ceremonies are marked by much rhythmic drumming and dancing, with devotees frequently falling into trances during which they are possessed by the voodoo gods, or loa.

A typical voodoo altar displays a colourful mix of fetishes, icons, symbols and figurines, with the top-hatted Baron Samadi often rubbing shoulders with the Virgin Mary. Voodoo priests and priestesses enjoy considerable prestige in the community and are often credited with powers of healing, prophecy and magic.

To most voodoo practitioners, the idea of creating a zombie is as repulsive as it is to the rest of us, but there are secret cults within voodoo which not only practise zombification, but actually use it to punish those they consider wrongdoers.

The author Wade Davis visited Haiti in 1984–85 in an attempt to discover how they did it. He was eventually invited to witness a ceremony devoted not to creating a zombie, but to creating something called "zombie powder" which could be used to reanimate the dead. The powder was cooked up in a graveyard at midnight. The priest mixed grave dust with powdered human bones and various other unsavoury ingredients like dead toads and sand crabs. Spells were chanted to empower the powder.

Davis could see little reason why the mixture might be expected to reanimate a corpse, but several of the ingredients raised his suspicions. Both the toads and the sand crabs were of highly poisonous species and the powder was completed by the addition of a secret ingredient added privately before the ceremony.

With considerable difficulty, Wade Davis managed to buy a sample of the powder and had it chemically analysed. Apart from the ingredients he already knew about, the report showed the presence of a hugely dangerous nerve poison called tetrodotoxin.

He knew at once where it had come from. Tetrodotoxin is found in the bones of puffer fish, easily obtainable in Haiti. The effect of puffer fish poison is quite well-known. Although hundreds of times more deadly than cyanide, tetrodotoxin does not kill immediately. It first produces a prolonged death-like trance in which the victim lies paralysed, but conscious, exactly like Andre Ville Jean-Paul. Bodily functions are so profoundly depressed as to be virtually undetectable and many victims of puffer fish poison are taken for dead and buried before death actually claims them.

Here, then, was the clue to the real secret of the zombie powder. The grave dust, spells and ground-up human bones were all so much window-dressing. It was the tetrodotoxin (combined with the poisonous toads and crabs) that really did the trick. A young, strong victim would be selected by the cult and secretly fed the powder. As the powerful poisons took effect, he would fall into the death trance. Believing him to be really dead, his family would rush to get him buried before the body began to smell.

A cult member would note the location of the grave and once the mourners went home, the "corpse" would be dug up again and an antidote given. This would neutralize the paralysing effects of the poisons, but leave the victim in a highly suggestible – sometimes even brain-damaged – state where he would obey orders without question … and work without pay on the zombie plantations of Haiti.

1. Voodoo drumming influences anybody who listens to it, not just believers, due to a process scientists call entrainment. This is the tendency for human brain waves to synchronize themselves to a rhythmic stimulus. With the right sort of beat, trance frequently follows – one of the reasons why people sometimes dance to the point of exhaustion at night clubs.

2. In Japan, puffer fish are considered a gourmet delicacy, especially by young (and not so young) men determined to impress their girlfriends with their courage.

Specially licensed restaurants employ highly trained chefs with the experience and skill to prepare the fish for the table. It is then served raw and thinly sliced as sushi. But if the chef misses even the tiniest toxic bone or sinew, the customer won't be coming back for second helpings ... ever. (As happened to three unfortunate Nagasaki diners in 1992.)

3. Not all zombies are animated corpses. Voodoo practitioners actually believe in two distinct types of zombie – the other being a disembodied spirit used for magical purposes.

4. The main Christian denomination in Haiti, the Roman Catholic Church, fought vigorously against voodoo for many years, even going so far as to advocate the persecution of its followers. But since its followers constitute about 80% of the Haitian population, this turned into a lost cause and the Church now pursues a policy of co-existence.

5. One reason for the particular loathing most people feel at the idea of a zombie is their long-time fear of being buried alive. This was particularly strong in Victorian times when patents were granted for several alarm devices which, when fitted to your coffin, allowed you to signal that you had been buried far too soon. Although actual live burial was extremely rare, the fear of it was widespread.

77

The Sons Who Are
Older Than Their Mother

Lots of people believe in reincarnation and some even claim to remember past lives. But Jenny Cockell went one better. Having recalled a past life as Dubliner Mary Sutton, who died in 1932, Jenny set out to find surviving members of her family...

Ireland, 1990

Since she was a little girl, Jenny Cockell, a chiropodist from Northamptonshire, was certain she had lived before. She was surprised that other people did not mention their past lives and didn't have the same ideas as herself.

As a child, there was nothing Jenny could do about the weird feelings that came over her. As she got older, she came to realize most of the people around her not only lacked any memory of their own past lives, but thought the whole idea of reincarnation was nonsense.

Jenny grew up and tried to get on with her life, pushing away the disturbing memories as best she could. But when her own children were born, the feelings associated with her past life memories began to emerge again even more strongly. At least part of this feeling arose out of a recurrent nightmare that she was dying. But it wasn't death that frightened her. In her dream, she was desperately worried about what would happen to the children she was leaving behind.

Throughout her own childhood, she had glimpses of a life in Ireland connected with the person she'd been in her dream. She took to drawing maps of the locality in which she'd lived. The maps became almost an obsession. She drew them over and over again.

Finally, she decided she might find the village she remembered if she looked at a detailed map of Ireland. Jenny found one and studied it carefully. Sure enough, she found herself attracted to Malahide, a village just to the north of Dublin. Despite her convictions, she had a creepy feeling when she found that Malahide matched the drawings she had made.

She decided she had to investigate further and, if possible, travel to Ireland. While she was saving for the trip, a friend put her in touch with a past lives researcher and in 1988 they embarked on a series of experiments involving something called hypnotic regression.

Hypnotic regression dates back to Sigmund Freud, the founding father of modern psychiatry. Freud discovered many emotional problems were rooted in long-forgotten childhood experiences and felt it was a doctor's job to help patients remember them. To this end, he developed a number of techniques – including hypnosis – to *regress* patients back to their early days.

If you're ever regressed to an early age, you'll find your vocabulary becomes limited and you may even begin to speak in a childlike voice. Personality changes will occur. Your behaviour becomes that of the suggested age level. If you're asked to do a drawing, it will look like the drawing of a little child. Even your handwriting will change and if you happen to have any samples of your writing at the early age, you'll find it matches up exactly.

At first, regressions stopped at childhood. But then, in 1898, a French practitioner named Albert de Rochas decided to find out if it was possible to regress someone beyond their birth. Soon his patients were reporting memories of experiences within the womb. Eventually de Rochas made the ultimate jump. His subjects were regressed *beyond* the womb. Surprisingly, they reported recollections of what appeared to be past lives.

When Jenny Cockell was regressed she was immediately flooded with memories, both during the hypnosis and between sessions. The memories recalled the life of a woman named Mary Sutton from Malahide, who had died in 1932 in the Rotunda Hospital in Dublin, leaving behind eight young children. Mary's husband had been a soldier during the First World War and afterwards earned a meagre living as a scaffolder.

The memories were so vivid, Jenny decided to find out if they were real. The only way she could do so was to mount an investigation in Ireland itself. When Jenny made her first visit to Ireland in 1989 she discovered there had indeed been a Sutton family in Malahide. Nor was it just a coincidence of name: the family matched her memories. Baptismal and orphanage records in Dublin confirmed Jenny's own memory of how many children there were. Her research confirmed they had been scattered after Mary's death.

It occurred to Jenny that some members of Mary's family might well still be alive – although they would be in their 60s and 70s – so she put a notice in the local paper appealing for information.

In 1990, Mary's second son, Jeffrey, made contact and over the following two years she found all but one of the other children.

It took the family quite a while to accept the possibility that Jenny had been their mother – after all she was *more than 30 years younger* than Sonny, Mary's eldest son. But Jenny could recall so many small details of their life together that the evidence became overwhelming.

An old photograph of Mary shows that she bore a striking physical similarity to Jenny. When a priest was consulted by one of the children, he said that as reincarnation was unacceptable to the Roman Catholic Church, perhaps the spirit of Mary was acting through Jenny to reunite the family.

Whatever the true explanation may be, for Jenny the nightmares are over.

FACT FILE

1. There are many cases similar to that of Jenny Cockell from all over the world. Shanti Devi, Bishin Chand and Reena Gupta in India, Joey Verwey in South Africa and Romy Crees in the United States are among the many youngsters who started to recall past lives and gave hard, detailed information that was later proven to be factually accurate.

2. Some Biblical scholars insist the early Christians believed in reincarnation. They base this on evidence such as the passage in Matthew 16, where Jesus asks his disciples who men said he was. The answer he got was that, "Some say that thou art John the Baptist: some, Elias; and others, Jeremiah, or one of the prophets." This, say the scholars, clearly points to a belief in reincarnation among the disciples, although the belief was not necessarily shared by Jesus himself.

3. As a child, Lebanon's Imad Elawar started to claim he'd lived before as somebody called Ibrahim Bouhamzy in a village called Khriby about 30 kilometres from Imad's home. One day Imad bumped into somebody he recognized from his past life, a man who actually was from Khriby. And when they questioned this character, they discovered he was a neighbour of ... Ibrahim Bouhamzy. That gave Imad's family

the incentive to investigate and they very quickly discovered that of 47 items of information given by Imad about the Bouhamzy family, 44 were absolutely accurate.

4. Dr Arthur Guirdham, formerly Chief Psychiatrist for Bath, had one patient who remembered a past life in France as a cathar – a heretic sect persecuted and eventually brutally stamped out by the orthodox church. At the time the information emerged, very little was known about this sect and several details given by the woman were held by historians to be inaccurate. But research over the following decade soon established the woman's memory was right and the historians were wrong. The details she had given were verified by subsequent discoveries.

5. There is fascinating evidence that regression may involve something more than simple memory. One subject, who had worn glasses since the age of 12, was regressed to the age of seven with a measurable improvement in vision – a development most opticians would insist was quite impossible. Another had been blind in the left half of the right eye, due to the presence of a cyst. When the cyst was surgically removed, his sight returned to normal. But when regressed to a time before the operation, the visual defect reappeared.

6. Although the major Western religions all deny the possibility of reincarnation, researchers have found almost without exception that people subjected to regression techniques undergo experiences that seem to be past life memories. Even atheists with no belief in survival after death sometimes remember "past lives". But not all these memories are accurate. There is conclusive proof that in some cases they were based on information from books the subject had read years before and forgotten.

THE WEIROZONE 3

Just when you thought it was safe to come out of the weirdness, here we go again. Prepare yourself for our next-to-last plunge into the Weird Zone...

Suicidal Spud

German scientists have invented a suicidal potato. The tuber's cells automatically shut down when attacked by potato blight. The idea is that potatoes of this sort will stop the spread of blight, thus saving the overall crop.

Paperwork

A 77-year-old American, Robert Shields of Washington State has (so far) produced a 38 million-word diary. The document is stored in 81 cardboard boxes and deals with each five minutes of his waking day. Entries include things like how many sheets of paper he used on a particular visit to the loo.

What's in a Name?

In Canada in 1996 there were allegations of election fraud following the discovery that Omar Sharif and Martina Navratilova were registered as voters in Old Montreal ... and both were living in the same apartment.

It turned out, however, both names were genuine. Omar is the son of the famous Egyptian film star and his wife Martina, while not the former Wimbledon tennis champion, uses her actual maiden name of Navratilova in her career as a stockbroker.

Unsettled Outlook

Israeli weatherman Danny Rup found himself facing a lawsuit in March 1996, because he got a forecast wrong. A female viewer of Channel Two where Danny works claimed she believed his prediction of sunshine and was caught in a downpour that gave her 'flu and made her miss four days' work.

Elvis Lives, Sort Of (1)

Thirty-one new Commandments were announced in 1996 by Ministers of the First Presleyterian Church of Elvis the Divine (founded 1988). They include exhortations to eat six meals a day and fight the anti-Elvis, Michael Jackson.

Elvis Lives, Sort Of (2)

The *Dundas Review*, a Canadian publication based in Ontario, ran a story backing the claim of a local singer that he was the reincarnation of Jesse Presley, stillborn twin brother of the famous Elvis. The singer, who works under the stage name Danny Boy, said God gave him life in order to continue Elvis's gospel work.

Definitely Dead

Kentucky ambulance drivers have been rushing corpses to hospital in order to claim extra fees from the county, according to a local coroner. One patient had been dead so long rigor mortis had set in and he couldn't even be fitted on a stretcher.

For Heaven's Saki

Japan's popular alcoholic tipple, *saki*, is best enjoyed at blood heat ... which has encouraged the Triumph Lingerie Company to develop a speciality bra containing about 40cc of saki in a waterproof pocket. When the bra is worn, the saki warms up to the right drinking temperature in about an hour.

Nice Work If You Can Get It (1)

Pete Springer who founded his company, Rats R Us, in California in 1993, sometimes gives mouth-to-mouth resuscitation to baby rodents to keep them alive. If he succeeds, the rats are sold as food for pet reptiles when they grow up.

Nice Work If You Can Get It (2)

According to the *Journal of Archaeological Science*, a research assistant was fed boiled shrew then had his bowel movements analysed over a period of three days. His director was trying to discover whether small bones found in a dig had been excreted by a larger animal. (They hadn't. The experiment showed that if you eat boiled shrew, you digest it bones and all.)

Nice Work If You Can Get It (3)

A male prisoner was sent to a woman's jail in Oslo, Norway, during 1996 … and stayed there undetected for a fortnight despite two strip searches.

Asleep on the Job

Air New Zealand now allows cockpit crews to take naps on international flights so long as at least one member stays awake. Airline instructions on how to wake sleeping crews insist they should not be startled.

ET Phone Home

A political science professor in the United States has published a book in which he claims to have talked to Jesus Christ, travelled in time, directly observed a distant galaxy and discovered a Martian civilization in New Mexico.

To Be or To Be

A Taiwanese couple in their middle 20s made a suicide pact when their parents refused to bless their wedding. They then tried to kill themselves by driving their car over a cliff, hanging themselves and jumping together from a 12-storey building, but failed each time.

Their parents have now given their blessing.

Fighting Back

When an ATM (cash-point machine) refused to give him money, 32-year-old Domenico Germano whipped out a gun and shot it four times. He got four years' probation and was ordered to pay the bank $5,000 in damages.

The Play's the Thing

When a prison theatre group went on tour in Italy in 1995 there was an abrupt rise in the crime rate. The authorities subsequently discovered that members of the group were robbing banks between shows, disguised in the make-up and costumes they wore on stage.

Are You Listening?
Canadians have been officially warned not to eat seafood that glows in the dark.

Beelieve it or Not
A swarm of bees invaded an airport in Norway during the summer of 1996 and grounded aircraft for almost three hours.

Proof Positive
In a divorce court in Albania, the plaintiff claimed his wife had beaten him regularly over the period of their two-year marriage. The wife was so enraged by his testimony that she jumped on him as he left the witness box and beat him unconscious before Court officials could drag her away. The divorce was granted.

Many Humps Make Light Work
In Australia, a town council has ordered that local camels must be fitted with tail lights.

Unlucky Day
Fifty-eight worshippers were crushed to death in two Hindu shrines in India during July 1996. They were seeking divine protection having discovered that the day was astrologically unlucky.

That's a Relief
You can now insure yourself against being abducted by aliens. A London broker has announced a policy that pays out if you are captured by extraterrestrials and pays out double if you become pregnant as a result. Interestingly, the pregnancy clause will still hold good for male policy-holders since the

extent of alien powers is currently unknown. Somebody in Essex has already been paid £1,000,000 under a policy of this type.

The Hopi Haunting

When two American treasure-hunters stole religious artefacts from a Native American reservation, it was a disaster for the Hopi Indians who lived there. But not half so much a disaster as faced the treasure-hunters themselves...

Arizona, USA, 1978

In July 1978 two Arizona treasure hunters stole four wooden figures from a cave above the village of Shungopavi within the Hopi Indian Reservation. Their greed and ignorance was to cost them more dearly than they could have imagined. But it also threatened the very soul survival of the few thousand remaining Hopi people.

The Hopi have always been one of the most peaceful and spiritual of all the Native American tribes and the stolen figures, called *taalawtumsi*, were believed to be living entities, essential to the crucial *stotokya* rite, when young Hopi men were initiated into manhood. The figures themselves represented Dawn Woman, Corn Maiden, Corn Maiden's Husband and Corn Maiden's Daughter.

The looters, Jimmy Lee Hinton and Randall Doyle Morris, thought they would make some easy money from a greedy art market. Keeping only the three largest figures – they threw away Corn Maiden's Daughter near the cave – they eagerly went searching for a buyer.

But after months of gallery visits, they gradually began to face up to the fact that no one would touch the artefacts. As the figures had never been seen by anyone but Hopi priests, the dealers thought they might be fakes.

Then things started to go wrong for the thieves at a much more personal level. Hinton became dangerously ill with kidney, liver and gall bladder failure. Morris was left without the use of an arm and a leg after a near-fatal motor cycle accident. Despite their health problems, the two continued to try to sell their stolen goods. Finally the figures were bought a private collector in August 1979 for US $1,600.

The money was of little benefit to the thieves. Both Hinton and Morris were jailed during the following two years, Hinton on a drugs charge and Morris for breaking the law on archaeological finds. Meanwhile, the agent who had bought the figures on behalf of the private collector died after months in a coma following a car crash.

When he got out of jail, Hinton returned with a couple of friends to the Hopi reservation for another treasure-hunting expedition. It was a weird decision. A Chicago art dealer had by this time warned him about the sacred power embodied in the Hopi figures and he must at least have wondered about the misfortunes that befell his partner and himself following his last theft. But whatever his motivation, Hinton went ahead.

There followed a night of sheer terror. The thieves became separated and each was haunted by strange lights and weird sounds. When they found each other the following morning, gibbering with fear, Hinton decided that he must be cursed and had to confess the theft of the *taalawtumsi* to break it.

Thefts from Native American reservations are a federal offence investigated not by the local police but by the FBI. Because Hinton never knew the name of the buyer, it was 1990 before the FBI traced him through another, quite unrelated, incident. His name was Eugene Pyle.

Pyle told the agents he had chopped up the figures and burnt them ten years earlier when he feared – wrongly as it turned out – that the FBI were on to him over the missing Hopi *taalawtumsi*. The FBI agreed not to prosecute on two conditions. The first was that he took a lie-detector test to confirm his story was true. The second was that he should tell his story to the Hopi people himself to show them the FBI had solved the case.

In March 1991 Pyle went to Shungopavi but many of the tribal elders, who still heard the spirits of their missing gods speak to them, could not believe they had been destroyed. Jimmy Lee Hinton was still haunted by Hopi images in his dreams and said he believed that "the *taalawtumsi* are out there, somewhere."

FACT FILE

1. The origins of the Hopi are unknown. According to their own mythology, their ancestors climbed up through four underground chambers and lived in many different places before reaching their present locations. Archaeology has since confirmed there were indeed many settlements before they reached their present settlement on the edge of the Painted Desert in Arizona.

2. The Hopi language has attracted a great deal of attention from linguists because of the way it expresses concepts of time and space, which it links together. In the 1930s, Benjamin Lee Whorf used Hopi to illustrate his hypothesis that language closely governs our experience of reality. If so, the Hopi seem for centuries to have directly experienced the reality of space-time, a concept only introduced to the rest of us by Albert Einstein in his Theory of Relativity.

3. A common feature of coming-of-age initiation rites like those of the Hopi disrupted by the theft of the sacred figures, is their emphasis on instruction. Youths learn about the behaviour appropriate to their new status as adults, as well as information on dress, speech, morality and secret matters of religion. Without such rites, the essential culture of a tribe can collapse completely over a few generations.

4. The most famous of all curses involved the opening, in 1927, of the Egyptian Pharaoh Tutankhamun's tomb. As archaeologist Lord Carnarvon stepped into the tomb, a mosquito bit him, he sickened and died. Expedition leader Howard Carter's partner, Richard Bethell, keeled over a few weeks later. His father, Lord Westbury, committed suicide. Colonel Herbat, one of those who entered the tomb with Carter, died unexpectedly. So did Jonathan Carver, who was also with them. When they took out Tutankhamun's mummy, they turned it over to Sir Archibald Douglas Reid to be x-rayed. He promptly died. Even Howard Carter's canary died. It was eaten by a python (Tutankhamun's symbol) the day he entered the tomb.

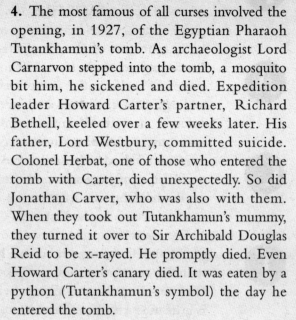

5. Curses often seem to cling to precious stones. The Koh-i-Noor diamond, now a part of the British crown jewels, was never lucky for India,

where it had an evil reputation. It brought greed, viciousness and misfortune on the Mogul kings who owned it. When Nadir Shah of Persia conquered Delhi in 1739, he took the stone and named it Koh-i-Noor or "mountain of light". Nadir Shah was murdered for the stone on his journey home and the diamond passed via further misfortune to Runjeet Singh who, on his deathbed, sent it for safekeeping to the Temple of Juggernaut. When the British annexed the Punjab in 1849 it was presented to Queen Victoria by the East India Company.

6. The use of curses seems to be as old as humanity itself, or at least as old as civilization. Kudurrus were a type of boundary stone used by the Kassites of ancient Mesopotamia to record a grant of land made by the king. But only clay copies of the kudurrus were actually used on the land. The originals were held in temples because the Mesopotamians believed this would automatically place a curse on anybody who trespassed.

Spontaneous Human Combustion

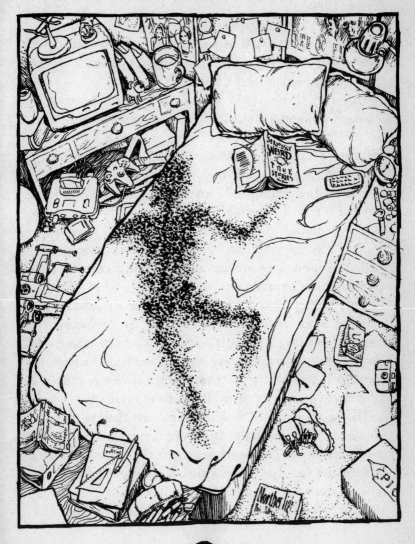

If it's chilly outside and you're wondering how on earth to get warm, thank your lucky stars you haven't (yet) fallen foul of one of the most terrifying weirdnesses ever to face the human race...

Wales, 1980

Human beings (as well as animals, accordions and other assorted objects) have been bursting into flames for no apparent reason throughout history.

This scary phenomenon, known as SHC (for Spontaneous Human Combustion), usually denounced as wild superstition, has produced several cases in recent years that have forced scientists to reassess their disbelief in the face of overwhelming – if somewhat grisly – evidence.

One of the leading UK investigators of SHC is John Heymer, a retired Scene-of-Crime Officer with Gwent CID. Not a credulous man and trained to assess facts with the greatest care, Heymer has collected some fascinating case studies – enough to convince him Spontaneous Human Combustion is seriously real.

On 6 January 1980, for example, Heymer was called to the scene of a domestic fire in Ebbw Vale, South Wales. He describes entering a living room lit by a strange orange-red glow. The room was radiating warmth and both the window and the light bulb were covered in a sticky orange-red substance. Greasy soot coated the walls and ceiling.

The knobs on the TV were melted and there were ashes from a coal fire in the grate. A partly burnt armchair was beside the fire and on the floor in between were the trousered remains of a leg and two feet at one end and a blackened skull at the other, surrounded by a great deal of ash. These tragic remains, all that was left of 73-year-old Henry Thomas, lay on a fitted carpet and part of the hearth rug. Both were charred only where they were touched by the ashes of the body.

In all normal cases of death by fire, the extremities of the human body burn first and the torso is left, because the mass of internal organs makes it the least combustible. But in the case of Henry Thomas, the fire appeared to have started in the torso itself. Like a bonfire, the fire eventually burnt out, leaving two of the extremities partially intact. This happened despite the fact the blaze was centred in the same place as the greatest concentration of water in the body – and water is usually known for putting fires out.

Nothing else in the room had caught fire. The room itself was so well sealed that the oxygen supply had been quickly used up. As far as science is concerned, nothing can burn without oxygen, so the fire could only have lasted a short time. The lack of oxygen makes the intense burning of Mr Thomas's body even more mysterious. Just about everything else in the room was (theoretically) more combustible than his body. What's more, as any undertaker will confirm, even the most modern cremation techniques cannot completely reduce a human body to ashes.

Even more weird was the fact that the ordinary plastic floor tiles beneath the carpet were completely undamaged while the torso and bones on the carpet were reduced to ashes.

Despite the peculiarities of the case, forensic experts preferred to believe that Mr Thomas had fallen head first into the grate, set fire to his head, then sat back down in his chair and waited quietly to burn to death. This was how they actually couched their report, despite the fact that there was no evidence Mr Thomas had fallen into the fire at all.

An inquest later suggested that the fire had been a routine accident probably caused by a spark or a dropped cigarette. Mr Thomas was a non-smoker.

1. As the human body is about 70% water, the average person would contain about 170 litres – of fluid, making it near miraculous that a body can burn all the way through at all.

2. The phenomenon of Spontaneous Human Combustion is far from new. A search through historical records shows that it was known in the Middle Ages and even as far back as ancient Greece and Rome where it was believed to be caused supernaturally by "fire from heaven".

3. One investigator of SHC unearthed evidence of three cases occurring simultaneously in the south of England. When plotted on a map they formed an equilateral triangle.

4. In Victorian Britain, three friends were out for a seaside walk when the one in the middle suddenly erupted in a pillar of flame, burning so fiercely that his companions were unable to approach him, let alone help. This is one of the very few cases where SHC occurred in the presence of witnesses.

5. Although not all investigators are as blind to the facts as the forensic experts quoted in Mr Thomas's story, there are real problems in explaining the phenomenon, which seems to defy the laws of chemistry. One ingenious suggestion is that iodine in sweat may combine with ammonia in the urine to precipitate a highly volatile chemical known as fulminate of ammonia. The difficulty with this theory is that fulminate of ammonia explodes violently rather than burning.

6. Water does not seem effective against SHC, but the fire can apparently be smothered if action is taken quickly enough. In one case study, the victim reported a small blue flame that leaped without warning out of his arm and burned fiercely, although without giving him pain. Instinctively he clamped his hand over it ... and the fire went out.

Loony Moon

Early science fiction writers sometimes described life on the moon. Today, of course, we know our satellite to be a lifeless body without atmosphere or activity. Or do we…?

Various places and dates

Astronomers are confident they know almost all there is to know about the moon. It is seen as a rocky body, possibly with a small metal core, that has no global magnetic field, no atmosphere worth considering, and no internal activity like earthquakes or volcanic eruptions. We see it shining only by reflected sunlight, generating neither light nor heat.

Most scientists now believe the moon was formed when a Mars-sized body struck Earth early in the history of the solar system, throwing a cloud of fragments into orbit. After a time, these came together to form the moon. It is now, and always has been, devoid of life and any signs of activity whatsoever.

The only thing wrong with this confident astronomical picture is that it doesn't fit the facts.

Back in 1884 astronomer John Haywood reported "a misty light" on the dark side of the moon similar to the Northern Lights on Earth. He and other observers saw the light twice in November of that year, again in December and twice more during March 1885. The light appeared in different places on the moon's surface.

In 1933, the First and Third Officers of the SS *Transylvania* recorded their observations in the ship's meteorological log of an orange ray projected up from the moon's surface.

These are just two examples from a multitude of reports claiming to observe lights on the surface of the moon. These have varied in size, location and colour. In 1946, the periodical *Science* recorded a sighting of what appeared to be lightning (which was, of course, impossible). In 1959, Soviet astronomers reported volcanic activity (which was, of course, impossible). In 1964 came news that Japanese observers had spotted a spreading pink patch (which was, of course, impossible).

One of the most intriguing reports, dating back to 1956, was that of Californian observer Robert Miles, who saw a flashing light on the edge of the Mare Crisium, a large crater on the moon. On 17 January, he watched the light which changed intermittently from white to blue for an hour and a half.

What (or who?) was sending signals from the moon? Scientists are dismissive of the possibility that anything might be living on our satellite – so dismissive that it is automatically ruled out of any theories they put forward. Yet in 1912, Frank B. Harris reported in the magazine *Popular Astronomy* that he had observed an "intensely black body" hovering above the surface of the moon.

Natural phenomena like meteors do not hover, so the nature of the intensely black body remains a profound mystery. These and similar sightings have led more maverick observers to speculate romantically about spaceships. But if Mr Harris was watching an alien craft in 1912, it was a very big one. He calculated that the black body was about 250 miles long and 50 miles wide.

The various manned and unmanned moon landings of the late 60s and early 70s did nothing to explain the vast collection of lunar mysteries that has gathered since the day Galileo developed the first telescope early in the 17th century. If anything they added more. Surveyor V and VI missions reported a bright line of light on the lunar horizon shortly after sunset – sightings that were subsequently confirmed by Surveyor VII. This "afterglow", which can last anything up to two hours, seems to be a regular phenomenon and has now been photographed.

If it occurred on Earth, there would be no problem – we would recognize that the last remnants of sunlight were simply reflecting off water and dust particles in the atmosphere. But the moon doesn't have an atmosphere, so the afterglow remains a mystery.

Except, that is, to Richard C. Hoagland, who in 1993 won the Angstrom Foundation's First International Angstrom Medal for Excellence in Science for his work on hyper-dimensional physics and its technological implications. Hoagland's analysis of NASA photographs showing the afterglow and several anomalous structures on the surface of the moon has led him to stake his reputation on the theory that what we are looking at is the last remnants of a gigantic glass dome which once covered vast areas of the lunar surface.

Despite its almost unimaginable size, he has no doubts the dome is artificial and represents the remains of an alien colony established on our satellite at some time in the depths of human prehistory…

FACT FILE

1. The moon is the closest astronomical body to Earth, orbiting at a mean distance of just under 400,000 kilometres.

2. By a weird coincidence, the moon spins on its axis at exactly the same rate as it orbits the Earth. This means that it always presents the same face to our planet.

3. Among the most peculiar discoveries of the Apollo 11 mission was that small lunar craters (that's to say no more than a couple of metres across) often contain lumps of soil coated with glass. There are also a great many small glass beads in the lunar soil itself.

4. A microparticle detector left on the moon by the Apollo 17 astronauts has gathered evidence of dust storms on the moon. Nobody has the least idea how they could possibly be caused.

5. Careful measurements of the lunar orbit seem to point to the conclusion that the Earth–moon system may not be stable. The moon's orbit appears to be expanding faster than it should, leading some astronomers to speculate that its gravitational pull is weakening.

6. In the 1930s, many German astronomers subscribed to the theory (supported by the ruling Nazi Party) that our present moon was only the latest in a series of satellites that once orbited our planet. The others eventually spiralled into the Earth, causing earthquakes, tidal waves and similar planetary catastrophes, including the Biblical Flood.

THE WEIRDZONE 4

There's no let-up. The strangeness just goes on and on. Nowhere in the world is safe – as you'll discover when you take your final dip into the Weird Zone…

Beats Revision

A force of more than 100 police officers ringed a school in Cambodia's capital, Phnom Penh, in an attempt to stamp out cheating in the secondary school entrance examinations. They were ignored by hundreds of children who climbed the walls to pass notes to their friends inside.

Graffiti Goes International

Louts in Germany who specialize in spray-painting graffiti on walls have taken to making pilgrimages to New York, which they believe to be the source site of their craft.

Hell Hath No Fury…

Pavulupitiyage Gunapala, an energetic Sri Lankan, has married 15 (simultaneous) wives despite the fact that bigamy is against the law in his country. The latest in this lengthy line reported him to the police on the grounds that he was unfaithful. When arrested, Pavulupitiyage proved to have written love letters to a further 54 women.

Naked Truth

Thirty-year-old Julian Carlo Fagotti decided to try for election to Curitiba City Council in summer 1996. He launched his election campaign with an appearance on Brazilian TV wearing nothing but one of his own brochures to cover his embarrassment.

Highly Trained
A US marine corporal stationed in Japan was dared by friends to stick his head in front of a speeding goods train. He did so and was knocked unconscious.

Nothing Personal
The Zimbabwe authorities are having real difficulty finding a replacement for their state hangman, who retired recently at the age of 72. The trouble is a superstition in the country which says it's bad luck to take somebody's life unless you have a personal motive. Their last hangman, Tommy Griffiths, was English.

Power of Prayer
The world's weirdest contract has just been signed between the Exiton Company and a group of Eastern Orthodox monks from Moldova, Eastern Europe. The contract specifies that Exiton will help the monks find some lost icons and support their monastery. The monks for their part are contracted to pray for Exiton's profits.

Bless Me, Computer, For I Have Sinned
Catholics can now confess to their computers. A new CD-ROM has been released in Germany which lists 200 of the most usual sins and prescribes appropriate penalties for each. Imaginative sinners who can't find their particular peccadillo on the list can customize the program to suit their own misdeeds. The CD, which is published by The Lazarus Society of Cologne, offers Internet links to real priests as a spiritual bonus.

Naked Ape
Human beings have gone on display in a zoo at Copenhagen, Denmark. A young couple now spend their days in a glass-walled natural habitat similar in most respects to a modern home. The display forms part of the zoo's primate collection.

Hair Today
An Australian artist has successfully sued her hairdresser for giving her a bad haircut. She was awarded $750 and allowed a further $234 compensation for the hats she had to buy to hide it.

Bouncing Czech
Chief Executive of the Czech Republic's Agrobanka was quick to welcome a raid which netted robbers the equivalent of about £6,000. He said it was a sign of public confidence that the bank actually had money in it now.

Keep on Truckin' (1)
Gamblers in an Oregon casino continued to play the slot machines for an hour, roundly ignoring the body of Arthur Mooney, who collapsed and died while on the premises.

Keep on Truckin' (2)
Four golfers in Scotland continued their round of golf after their companion, Jimmy Hogg, died of a heart attack at the first hole. The game was interrupted only long enough for an ambulance to take the body away.

Silly Moo
Miss South Africa, Peggy-Sue Khumalo, announced she planned to mark her winning of the title by sacrificing a goat

to her ancestors. Fortunately, she failed to make the Miss World title two months later despite having promised to sacrifice a cow and ten oxen.

Barking Mad

A very special package holiday is now in its seventh year in Vermont, USA. The two week long holiday costs $1,300 but includes square dancing, swimming lessons, Frisbee catching and a bathing suit pageant ... all for dogs.

Disabled Enterprise

An attempt by a legless man to hold up a bank in Frankfurt, Germany, was foiled when a quick-witted customer tipped over his wheelchair.

Weight Loss

Over a period in the 1920s, a macabre series of experiments was carried out by Dr Duncan McDougall of Haverhill, Massachusetts, who decided to *weigh* those of his patients who were in the process of dying from tuberculosis. He placed them, bed and all, on a delicately balanced scale ... and waited. As death occurred, he discovered, in four out of six cases, a weight loss varying between two and two-and-a-half ounces.

Mind Over Matter

The death was recently announced of a Russian woman, Nina Kulagina, who seemed capable of moving matchsticks, compass needles, fountain pens and other small objects simply by concentrating on them. She passed intensive tests in both Soviet and American laboratories and on one occasion caused a journalist's half-eaten sandwich to crawl across the table during an interview.

Crime Wave

An arrest in a Minnesota shopping mall uncovered evidence of a crime wave. Police first arrested a man on suspicion of snatching a valuable gold chain. They then arrested a witness when a computer check showed he was wanted for several crimes. Finally they arrested the victim, who was carrying drugs.

Court Battle

Prosecutor Michael Spivack and defence lawyer Howard Sohn lost their tempers in a Miami court and started wrestling with each other. Sohn got Spivack in a headlock and repeatedly rammed his head against the jury-room door before they could be separated. Unmindful of the trial, jurors began taking bets on the outcome of the fight.

Court Ruling

It's now law in both Somalia and Afghanistan that men must wear beards.

Woman From Atlantis

As she was pulled from the Atlantic Ocean about two miles from the nearest land, a fully-dressed woman told her would-be rescuers, "I'm fine – my family is here." She claimed to have been underwater for three days, eating seaweed, and had just come up for air.

They Don't Make Men Like That Any More (1)

A single-engined aeroplane was coming in to land at an Australian airfield when its pilot, 51-year-old Brian Howson, discovered there was something wrong with the landing gear. Howson promptly hung out of the door of his plane at 4,000 feet to repair the gear while three passengers clung to his legs. The plane landed safely.

They Don't Make Men Like That Any More (2)

Texan Valentin Grimaldo was bitten by a poisonous coral snake while enjoying the great outdoors. He reacted by biting the snake's head off, skinning it, then using the skin as a tourniquet until help arrived.

Afterword

Several of the seriously weird case studies you've just finished reading are historical – indications that weirdness has never been a stranger to this planet, however far back you go. But it's probably only in your lifetime (or at most in your parents' lifetime) that weirdness has become enshrined in science.

Take physics, for example. In that most sober of sciences, practitioners deal happily, even routinely, with stuff that drives any normal person nuts the minute they start to think about it. Below are just a few examples.

The neutrino is a subatomic particle with almost no measurable characteristics. It has no mass, electric charge, or magnetic field. It is not subject to gravity, or influenced by the electrical or magnetic fields of any other particles with which it may come in contact. It is, in short, a sort of disembodied spin. Accordingly, a neutrino can pass through any solid body – even a planet – as if it were empty space. One physicist remarked that if ghosts exist, neutrinos are the stuff they must be made of.

Light consists of streams of particles called photons. Photons, by definition, travel at the speed of light. But Einstein showed that at the speed of light, time stands still.

Einstein also showed that time and space aren't really separate, however we experience them. Which means that any particle moving at the speed of light can't actually exist in the universe as we know it. So how come you can read this book? Your eyes seem to be able to sense something beyond the known universe.

Although most physicists agree nothing can be accelerated beyond the speed of light, many of them are now trying to track down particles that came into existence travelling faster than the speed of light and thus didn't have to be accelerated. Called tachyons, the weirdest characteristic of these particles is that they would have to travel back through time.

And talking of time, we've long known that the actions we take today can, must and always will influence our future. But an experiment has now been carried out to prove conclusively that actions you take today can also influence the past. This makes no sense, of course, but then neither does the theory put forward by one scientist (the distinguished British astronomer Fred Hoyle) that you may wake up in a different universe each morning. But since your brain is programmed with a full set of memories appropriate to that universe, you have no way of knowing and will probably never notice.

There's worse. Physicists have discovered that when you get down beyond the atom, what you have isn't atomic fragments. What you have is ... nothing at all. Matter at bedrock seems to consist of patterns of probability and nothing else. Which means it isn't really there at all.

You live in this unreal universe, equipped from the moment of your birth with what appears to be a solid body. But your body is in the same category as the solidity of the world. If you could see it as it really is, most of your body consists of empty space. And even the atoms in it are constantly changing.

You renew your liver (completely) every few weeks. You expel part of your substance with every breath. You shed skin constantly in the form of flakes – if your friends' eyes turned into microscopes they would see you as a little snowstorm that never, ever stopped. Over the course of about a year, every molecule and fibre of your entire body has been replaced.

Scientists estimate that as you sit there, you contain about a million atoms from the body of Jesus Christ. Unfortunately, you also contain a million atoms donated by Adolf Hitler and a million more that belonged to Ghengis Khan. They jostle with atoms from distant stars, atoms from the depths of the sea, atoms spewed from volcanoes, atoms excreted by octopuses, atoms handed on by bluebottles and bedbugs.

The body you occupied when you started this book is a different body to the one you're using now to read these words.

Can life get much weirder than that?

Have you read . . .

SERIOUSLY WEIRD TRUE STORIES

by Herbie Brennan

Green children, unexplained time slips, strange stone circles, mysterious beasts . . . nine incredible tales and over a hundred weird facts.

Prepare to be seriously amazed.

TRUE

WAR

HORROR

GHOST

MONSTER

SURVIVAL

SHARK

CRIME

DETECTIVE

SPORT

UFO

STORIES